National Library of Canada Cataloguing in Publication

Duggan, Derm
    Jake and Jigger / by Derm Duggan.

ISBN 1-894463-29-3

    1. Canadian wit and humor (English)--Newfoundland and Labrador.
2. Newfoundland and Labrador--Humor.   I. Title.

PN6178.C3D876 2003   C818'.602   C2003-904418-1

Copyright © 2003 by Derm Duggan

ALL RIGHTS RESERVED. No part of the work covered by the copyright hereon may be reproduced
or used in any form or by any means—graphic, electronic or mechanical—without the written per-
mission of the publisher. Any request for photocopying, recording, taping or information storage
and retrieval systems of any part of this book shall be directed to the Canadian Reprography
Collective, 379 Adelaide Street West, Suite M1, Toronto, Ontario M5V 1S5. This applies to class-
room use as well.

Printed in Canada

Flanker Press Ltd.
P.O. Box 2522, Station C
St. John's, Newfoundland A1C 6K1
Toll Free: 1-866-739-4420
Telephone: (709) 739-4477
Fax: (709) 739-4420

E-mail: info@flankerpress.com
www.flankerpress.com

BY DERM DUGGAN

Flanker Press Ltd.
St. John's, Newfoundland
2003

JAKE, THE WIFE SAID TO ME, "I'M A
WOMAN OF FEW WORDS AND IF I
BECKON WITH MY FINGER THAT
MEANS COME, AND COME QUICKLY."

AND I SAID TO HER, "I'M A MAN
OF FEW WORDS MYSELF AND IF
I SHAKE MY HEAD THAT MEANS
I AIN'T COMING."

SO YOUR BROTHER-IN-LAW
LOST HIS JOB AS A BUTLER,
JIGGER.

YEAH, THEY TOLD HIM
TO CALL THE NAMES OF
ALL THE GUESTS AS THEY
ARRIVED AT THE PARTY.

WELL, COULDN'T
HE DO THAT?

YEAH, BUT SOME OF THE NAMES HE
CALLED THEM CAN'T BE REPEATED.

JAKE, HERE'S AN OLD
NEWFOUNDLAND SAYING...

I JUST MADE THIS UP:
NO MAN GOES BEFORE HIS
TIME, UNLESS OF COURSE
THE BOSS LEAVES EARLY.

3

JAKE, IT WAS ON WALL STREET THAT I LOST EVERY CENT I HAD.

IS THAT THE TRUTH, JIGGER?

YEAH, I WAS STANDING ON THIS VERY CORNER WHEN I STUMBLED AND FELL, DROPPING MY LAST LOONEY IN THE SEWER.

5

JAKE, I SAW SIX PEOPLE
STANDING UNDER AN
UMBRELLA AND NOT ONE
OF THEM GOT WET.

HOW COME NOBODY
GOT WET, JIGGER?

'CAUSE IT WASN'T
RAINING, I GUESS.

7

JAKE, GUESS WHAT? WE GOT A NEW BABY AT OUR HOUSE AND EVERYONE IS SOME EXCITED.

WHY, JIGGER, DID YOU TURN IN THE OLD ONE?

MY SISTER'S NEW BABY IS
JUST TWO AND A HALF WEEKS
OLD AND SHE'S COMING
OVER TO OUR HOUSE.

WHAT'S ITS
NAME, JIGGER?

I DUNNO, BOY. I
CAN'T UNDERSTAND
A WORD IT SAYS.

THE BOSS SAID WHEN HE HIRED ME IF I DID MY WORK WELL WE WOULD TALK ABOUT A RAISE.

AH WELL JAKE, I MIGHT HAVE KNOWN THERE'D BE A CATCH TO IT.

Y'KNOW JAKE, I ONCE HAD A JOB ASSEMBLING IN A PARACHUTING FACTORY.

DID YOU HAVE ANY PROBLEMS, JIGGER?

NO ONE HAS COMPLAINED OF A PARACHUTE NOT OPENING.

ME UNCLE WILL WAS
BEFORE COURT, BUT WHEN
THEY TRIED HIM THE
JUDGE LET HIM GO FREE.

THAT RIGHT, JIGGER?

YEAH, UNCLE WILL WAS DEAF AN' AS
ANYONE KIN TELL YOU, YOU CAN'T
CONVICT A MAN WITHOUT A HEARING.

WHERE DID YOUR COUSIN MEET HIS GIRL, JIGGER?

BELIEVE IT OR NOT, JAKE, HE MET HER IN A REVOLVING DOOR AND HE'S BEEN GOING AROUND WITH HER EVER SINCE.

I'M NOT AS STINGY AS MY
UNCLE – ONE DAY HE WAS
WALKING THROUGH THE
ALLEY AND HE FOUND ON THE
GROUND A PACKAGE FILLED TO
THE BRIM WITH UNTOUCHED
COUGH-DROPS.

SO WHAT DID HE
DO, JIGGER?

THAT NIGHT HE MADE HIS WIFE SLEEP
OUT IN THE GARDEN SO THAT SHE WOULD
CATCH A COLD.

JAKE, ON THINKING IT OVER, I MADE MY
DECISION TO REFUSE THE OFFER AS THE
PRESIDENT OF A BUSINESS COMPANY.

WHY DID YOU DO
THAT, JIGGER?

BECAUSE THERE WAS NO CHANCE
FOR ADVANCEMENT.

JIGGER, HOW DID YOU GET THAT BLACK EYE?

WELL JAKE, YOU KNOW
THAT BEAUTIFUL BLOND
WHOSE HUSBAND IS IN
CHINA?

WELL, HE ISN'T IN CHINA.

16

JAKE, I TOLD MAGGIE, "I'M
GOING TO KISS YOU TONIGHT
OR DIE IN THE ATTEMPT."

WELL JIGGER,
DID YOU?

YOU DIDN'T SEE MY NAME
IN THE OBITUARY COLUMN,
DID YOU?

JAKE, THE JUDGE ASKED
ME, "YOUNG FELLOW,
HAVE YOU EVER BEEN UP
BEFORE ME?"

AND I SAID, "I DON'T
KNOW, YER HONOUR,
WHAT TIME DO YOU
GET UP?

JIGGER, I'D LIKE TO KNOW IF I HAVE GROUNDS FOR A DIVORCE.

ARE YOU MARRIED, JAKE?

YES.

THEN OF COURSE YOU HAVE.

19

HE WAS TO GET A
MEDAL FOR BRAVERY
BUT THEY COULDN'T
GIVE IT TO HIM, JAKE.

WHY NOT,
JIGGER?

HE WAS SO UGLY THEY COULDN'T
FIND A FRENCH GENERAL WHO
WOULD KISS HIM.

I HEAR YOU TOOK
THAT CHORUS GIRL
OUT TO DINNER. WHAT
DID SHE HAVE?

SOUP, SALAD, FISH,
CHICKEN, DESSERT
AND COFFEE.

WHAT DID
YOU HAVE?

HEART FAILURE.

21

JIGGER, I JUST GOT A
NOTICE FROM THE BANK
SAYING I'M OVERDRAWN.

TRY SOME OTHER
BANK, JAKE. THEY
CAN'T ALL BE
OVERDRAWN.

22

WHAT CAN I DO
FOR YOU, JIGGER?

I WANT A HAT.

FEDORA?

NO, FOR ME.

WHEN I FIRST WENT TO
NEW YORK I HAD ONLY A
DOLLAR IN MY POCKET
WITH WHICH TO MAKE A
START.

JIGGER, HOW DID YOU
INVEST THAT DOLLAR?

USED IT TO PAY FOR A
TELEGRAM HOME FOR
MORE MONEY.

I CAME IN HERE TO
GET SOMETIHNG FOR
MY WIFE, JIGGER.

WHAT ARE YOU
ASKING FOR HER?

25

I ONCE STOLE
MONEY, JAKE.

WHERE DID YOU STEAL
IT FROM, JIGGER?

A BANK.

HOW MUCH DID YOU
STEAL?

A HALF DOLLAR.

WHAT BANK WAS IT?

MY BABY SON'S.

JAKE, I ASKED THE
JUDGE, "WHAT FLOOR IS
THIS, YOUR HONOUR?"
"THE FIFTH FLOOR," HE
SAID. "IN THAT CASE, I'M
GOING UPSTAIRS."

WHAT FOR?

I SAID, "I WANT TO BE
TRIED IN A HIGHER COURT."

THE JUDGE SAID,
"HAVE YOU A LAWYER?"

"NO," I SAID, "BUT I HAVE SOME
GOOD FRIENDS ON THE JURY."

JIGGER, WHAT ARE
YOU GOING TO GIVE
ME FOR CHRISTMAS?

CLOSE YOUR EYES AND
TELL ME WHAT YOU SEE.

NOTHING.

THAT'S WHAT YOU'RE GOING
TO GET FOR CHRISTMAS.

SEE THESE STOCKINGS, JAKE? I JUST PAID
FIVE DOLLARS FOR THEM. THEY'RE A GIFT
FOR MY GIRL. DO YOU THINK SHE'LL LIKE
THEM?

WHY, THERE'S A RUN IN
EACH STOCKING.

YEAH – I DID THAT – I WANTED TO GET
A RUN FOR MY MONEY.

YESTERDAY WHILE WE WERE OUT
HUNTING YOU ALMOST SHOT MY
MOTHER-IN-LAW, JIGGER

SORRY, HERE'S MY GUN.
TAKE A SHOT AT MINE.

HOW DID HE DIE?

HE PASSED AWAY DURING A
CARD GAME.

WHAT DID HE DIE OF?

FIVE ACES.

WELL JAKE, SOMETHING
TERRIBLE HAS HAPPENED TO ME.

I WAS WALKING ALONG WITH MY
FRIEND DAVID AND HE SAID,
"SOMEBODY IS FOLLOWING US."

"WHO IS IT?" I ASKED. DAVID SAID,
"I DON'T KNOW," AND THEN A MAN
CAME UP AND HANDED ME THIS
BIG PIECE OF PAPER."

AFFIDAVIT?

NO, HE WAS
AFTER ME.

JAKE, I ASKED MY GIRL'S FATHER WOULD HE CON-
SENT TO ME MARRYING HIS DAUGHTER AND HE
REPLIED, "I DUNNO, CAN YOU SUPPORT A FAMILY?"

WHAT DID YOU
SAY, JIGGER?

SO I SAID TO HIM, "I GUESS SO – HOW
MANY OF YOU ARE THERE?"

YA KNOW JAKE, ME AN' NELL HAVE BEEN MARRIED 10 YEARS AN' ME MOTHER-IN-LAW HAS ONLY VISITED US ONCE.

THAT RIGHT, JIGGER?

YEP, SHE CAME THE DAY AFTER WE WERE MARRIED AN' NEVER LEFT!

Y'KNOW JAKE, WE WERE
NEVER WHAT Y'CALL
WELL-OFF.

THAT RIGHT,
JIGGER?

WHEN I WAS OLD ENOUGH TO BUY ME OWN CLOTHES
I WALKED FROM ONE END OF WATER STREET TO THE
OTHER LOOKIN' FOR SHORTS WITH "ROBIN HOOD
FLOUR" PRINTED ON THEM.

JAKE, ME NEW EMPLOYER TOLD ME THAT MY
SALARY IS PERSONAL AND NOT TO BE DISCLOSED
TO ANYONE.

"DON'T WORRY ABOUT IT," I TOLD HIM, "I'M
JUST AS ASHAMED OF IT AS YOU."

I KNOWS WHAT
POOR IS...

THAT RIGHT,
JIGGER?

Y'KNOW JAKE, I WAS TWELVE YEARS OLD
BEFORE I KNEW A TURKEY HAD ANY
MORE THAN A NECK.

AH JAKE, I REMEMBERS WHEN IT WAS SO COLD IN OUR
HOUSE OUR NEXT DOOR NEIGHBOUR USED TO ASK
MUDDER IF SHE COULD PUT HER JELLY IN MY ROOM!

JAKE, YOU MIGHT NOT THINK OF ME AS HANDSOME, BUT EVERY DAY I'M ASKED TO GET MARRIED.

BY WHO, JIGGER?

ME MOTHER AND FATHER.

43

AH JAKE, SOME PEOPLE HAVE THE GIFT FOR
MAKING MONEY – EVERYTHING ME BRUDDER
TOUCHES TURNS TO GOLD.

THAT RIGHT,
JIGGER?

NOT ME THOUGH – EVERYTHING I TOUCHES
THEY MAKES ME PUT BACK.

JAKE, THE NEXT WOMAN I MARRY
WILL BE A WOMAN WHO CAN SEW...

Y'KNOW, THE KIND YOU CAN GIVE A HANDFUL
OF BUTTONS AN' SAY HERE, SEW SOME SHIRTS
ON THESE.

Y'KNOW JAKE, ONLY ONCE DID ANY
HOT WORDS PASS BETWEEN ME AN'
THE MISSUS.

THAT RIGHT,
JIGGER?

YEP, T'WAR WHEN SHE THREW A POT OF
ALPHABET SOUP AT ME.

JAKE, ME WIFE SAYS SHE DIDN'T HAVE A RAG ON HER BACK WHEN SHE MARRIED ME.
THAT RIGHT, JIGGER?
WELL, SHE GOT PLENTY OF THEM NOW.

JAKE, I TOLD MY WIFE THAT
WE SHOULD HAVE SOME FUN
THIS EVENING.

SHE SAID, "THAT'S GREAT HONEY, I'VE WANTED TO DO
THAT FOR A LONG TIME – I'LL REALLY ENJOY IT, AND IF
YOU GET HOME BEFORE ME, BE A DEAR AND LEAVE
THE LIGHT ON IN THE HALL."

JAKE, I NEED TO GET ONE HUNDRED AND SIXTY
SQUARE HOLES BY TUESDAY.

I NEEDS TO GET THEM FOR THIS WEEK I
PROMISED TO MAKE A FISH NET.

JAKE, MY WIFE AND MYSELF HAD A ROW TODAY
BECAUSE OF ME EATING WITH ME FINGERS

BUT I TOLD HER – IF THE FOOD WASN'T CLEAN
ENOUGH TO PICK UP WITH MY FINGERS THEN
IT WASN'T FIT TO EAT.

AH JAKE, WORK, WORK
ALL DAY LONG, FROM
MORN UNTIL LATE AT
NIGHT.

HOW LONG HAVE YOU
BEEN IN THAT JOB,
JIGGER?

WHO, ME? I STARTS TOMORROW.

THE JUDGE ASKED ME UNCLE IF HE
HAD ANYTHING TO OFFER THE
COURT BEFORE HE WAS TO BE
SENTENCED.

AND WHAT DID YOUR
UNCLE SAY, JIGGER?

HE SAID, "NO YOUR HONOUR, MY
LAWYER TOOK MY LAST DOLLAR."

JAKE, MY WIFE IS COOKING AN
ENTHUSIASTIC STEW FOR SUPPER.

I CALLS IT ENTHUSIASTIC STEW BECAUSE SHE
PUTS EVERYTHING INTO IT.

JAKE, WHEN THE DAY IS FINISHED I REFUSE TO
TAKE MY TROUBLES TO BED.

YES B'Y, YOU SEE MY WIFE WON'T
SLEEP BY HERSELF.

JAKE, QUIT CALLING ME A HENPECKED NEWFIE
SHRIMP – BY JAPERS YOU WOULDN'T CALL ME
THAT IF MY MISSUS WERE HERE NOW.

Y'KNOW JAKE, I'VE FINALLY
TAKEN THE TIME TO WRITE
MYSELF A SERIOUS LETTER.

THAT'S FINE JIGGER,
WHAT DOES IT SAY?

HOW THE HECK DO I KNOW? I WON'T
GET IT UNTIL TUESDAY!

Y'KNOW JAKE, I DON'T KNOW WHO I
AM – I WAS LEFT ON THE NUN'S
DOORSTEP WHEN
I WAS A LITTLE BABY.

THAT RIGHT,
JIGGER?

I WONDER IF I'M A BOTTLE OF MILK?

JAKE, MY SON WANTED ME TO MEET
HIM AT THE AIRPORT.

WELL, DID YOU?

AHH, NO B'Y. SURE I'VE KNOWN
HIM ALL ME LIFE.

AH JAKE, THINGS ARE SOME BAD
HERE IN CANADA – OH MY, OH MY.

HOW COME,
JIGGER?

SURE I WENT BANKRUPT THREE TIMES AND
DIDN'T MAKE A DIME EITHER TIME.

I'M NOT UP ON WOMEN'S FASHIONS. MY
WIFE ASKED ME IF I WOULD LIKE TO SEE
HER IN SOMETHING LONG AND FLOWING.

WHAT DID YOU TELL
HER, JIGGER?

I SAID, "GO JUMP IN RENNIES RIVER."

JAKE, I'M NOT WORKING HERE ANYMORE
BECAUSE ME AND THE BOSS HAD A DISAGREE-
MENT AND HE WON'T TAKE BACK WHAT HE SAID.

WHAT DID HE SAY, JIGGER?

YOU'RE FIRED!

JAKE, I HAD A GOOD SITUATION –
EASY WORK AND GOOD PAY.

I GAVE IT UP DUE TO ILLNESS – THE
BOSS IN CHARGE OF THE SHIFT
WORKERS GOT SICK OF ME.

JAKE, I ONCE HAD A DANDY WATCH. THREE YEARS AGO I DROPPED IT IN RENNIES RIVER. THEN ONE DAY I FOUND IT AND IT'S STILL RUNNING TO THIS DAY.

THE SAME WATCH?

NO, RENNIES RIVER.

AND NOW WE'LL HAVE A SNAKE DANCE –
GIVING ALL THOSE WHO SNAKED IN WITHOUT
PAYING THE CHANCE TO SNAKE OUT AGAIN.

JAKE, THE JUDGE THAT HEARD MY CASE WAS
NOT ONLY STUPID, BUT YOU COULD TELL
THAT HE WAS BLIND.

THREE TIMES HE ASKED, "WHERE'S MY HAT?" AND
THE WHOLE TIME IT WAS ON MY HEAD.

JAKE, I REALLY NEED TO SEE A DOCTOR. I CAN'T EVEN REMEMBER WHAT HAPPENED YESTERDAY!

HOW LONG HAVE YOU HAD THIS PROBLEM, JIGGER?

WHAT PROBLEM?

JIGGER, HOW COME YOU REALLY HAVE
NO TIME FOR PETE?

WELL JAKE, I DON'T LIKE HIM AT ALL. IF YOU WERE
DROWNING, HE'S THE KIND OF FELLOW WHO WOULD
THROW YOU BOTH ENDS OF THE ROPE.

JAKE, THE JUDGE ASKED ME IF I WANED TO
CHALLENGE ANY MEMBER OF THE JURY.

SO I TOLD HIM, "YOUR HONOUR, I THINK I COULD
LICK THAT LITTLE OLD MAN WITH THE BALD HEAD.

Y'KNOW JAKE, I FINALLY FIGURED OUT
THE REASON THAT I'M SO
DEPRESSED...I'M HOMESICK.

BUT JIGGER, THIS
IS YOUR HOME.

EXACTLY, I'M SICK OF IT.

TOO BAD ABOUT O'TOOLE. I THOUGHT HIS BUSINESS WAS BOOMING. HE MUST HAVE FAILED AND IS NOW ON WELFARE.

I JUST SAW HIM DRIVING A CADILLAC.